Healing Words

*55 Powerful Daily Confessions &
Declarations to Activate Your Healing &
Walk in Divine Health... Strong Decrees
That Invoke Healing for You & Your Loved
Ones*

DANIEL C. OKPARA

Table Of Contents

FREE BONUS …

Download These 4 Powerful Books Today for FREE... And Take Your Relationship With God to a New Level.

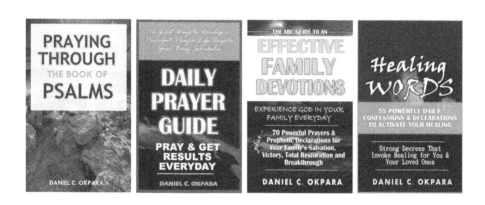

www.betterlifeworld.org/grow

Introduction

"Be mindful when it comes to your words. A string of some that don't mean much to you, may stick with someone else for a lifetime." **-Rachel Wolchin**

Words are spiritual forces that have power to create physical realities. This is not a mere new age philosophy. It is an infallible truth, etched in the WORD of God. By speaking a certain way, you can fast-track the manifestation of your healing which you have prayed for.

If you have read my book, **healing prayers**, you

would have known that I believe in divine healing. I believe that God's power can heal us of any ailment we face today. It doesn't matter how serious the matter is. It doesn't matter the name the doctors call it. God's power can set us free.

I have personally experienced supernatural healing several times in my life. So no one can talk me out of it. *I believe that we can pray and receive healing from heaven.* God doesn't count on our sins to heal us. We don't need to struggle to receive healing from God. All we need to do is...

- Pray

- Believe

- Speak the WORD and...

- Act the WORD

And we'll get healed.

In this book, which is a follow up to the book, Healing Prayers, I want to help you with WORDS you should be speaking after praying for healing to release God's healing power in your life or that of your loved ones.

If you have prayed and believe God for your healing, then start speaking these **words of healing** daily and you'll surely be made perfect in your health. If you have a loved one who is experiencing health challenges at the moment, forward this book to him/her and or help the person learn to speak these WORDS of healing.

It won't be long, the **WORDS of Healing** you

speak will form flesh and be made manifest as a light, total deliverance and restoration. It works. God's WORD works.

How to Speak The Healing WORDS.

"Your words have power. Speak words that are kind, loving, positive, uplifting, encouraging, and life-giving."

-Unknown

In each chapter of this book I present you with Words of Healing from God's WORDS and how to speak these Words for your healing, deliverance and total restoration. You can speak these words to yourself anytime, during the day or in the night.

You can copy the confessions out and memorize them and use them for self-talk, self-persuasion, self-discussion, self-ministration or whatever. If you are ministering to someone, help the person to make the confessions out loud until he can say it when you're not there.

The confessions are arranged in chapters, so you can flip to any chapter and the words in the chapter will speak to you and your health.

Always remember that the universe we live in today was created by WORDS....The WORDS of God. As an image of God you can create or recreate your life experiences with your OWN words. And when the words you speak are God's WORDS, you are guaranteed results.

Each chapter is arranged in the following style:

- **KICKER** (Short inspirational introduction to the chapter confession focus)

- **ASSURANCE** (What God says that you can hold onto as you make the confessions)

- **ATTITUDE** (What you are expected to do)

- **CONFESSIONS** (The recommended healing words/ confessions)

There are just about 5 confessions and declarations in each of the confession chapter page, so that you won't get bored with speaking these healing words. I highly recommend that you make these confessions morning and night. Choose two or four chapters each day and follow through with their **ATTITUDE** and **CONFESSIONS**. Before long your healing would be made manifest.

Some Things About Words You Should Know.

"Be careful with your words. Once they are said, they can be only forgiven, not forgotten." –Unknown

---

In an age where words seemingly spill out of us onto social networks, in presentations, in casual conversation, on blog comments and in the content we increasingly create and share with the world, are we giving our words enough forethought?

The words you use, whether verbally or in writing, can influence how others perceive you. They factor into the decisions people will make about you. They can build — or destroy — YOU and — your relationships.

"Words have power. Words are power. Words could be your power, "says public speaker, Mohammed Qahtani.

"The words you say every day, do not just affect others who hear it, it also affects you who say it. In fact, your words affect you the more."

It's not just Mohammed Qahtani and I who thinks that words have tremendous power. The Bible already has tons of suggestions and warnings on the power of words. Solomon, in the peak of his wisdom said, "*...death and life are in the power of the tongue and those who love it will eat the fruit of it (Proverbs 18:21)."*

Jesus said in Matthew 12:37 that...

"By thy words thou shalt be justified, and by thy words thou shalt be condemned."

Speaking the right words have been proven in different quarters to release the power to win various tough battles in life.

If you have access to the internet you may have read about the famous experiments of Dr. Masaru Emoto, a Japanese scientist and researcher. He became famous for his experiments on water and rice and their various responses to words, negative and positive.

The rice experiment in particular is interesting because sevcral non-science people have tried it and reported almost same results. The steps are like this:

1. Place 1 cup of Cooked Rice into three separate containers. Place a lid on each.

2. Mark one container with a positive phrase, like "Thank You Rice"

3. Mark the other container with a negative phrase, like, "You're an idiot."

4. Mark the other container with nothing, meaning, ignored.

4. Place them in your kitchen at least 12 inches apart.

5. Once or more every day, say aloud to the rice container the phrase written on it.

Figure 1: Illustrating Dr. Emoto's experiment (Caveat: Please note that I haven't tried this experiment myself and there are actually others who have written to disprove the experiment as untrue)...

It sounds nuts, but all those who have actually tried it have come back claiming results that are very similar. They have always reported that the jars produce results like:

"Thank You!" rice "began to ferment, giving off a strong, pleasant aroma."

The "You're An Idiot" rice turned mostly black, and the ignored rice "began to rot," turning a disgusting green-blue color.

According to Emoto, the "ignored" rice fared the worst because negligence and indifference are the absolute worst things we can do to water, rice...and ourselves. He goes on to explain that "we should converse with children," a piece of monumental parenting advice that is sure to forever be attributed to this rice experiment.

Positive words with good intentions behind them nurture and encourage healing and growth. Negative words with negative emotions literally rot and destroy.

The idea *that words can heal or destroy is actually beyond new age or rice talk.* There's even a simpler experiment for you to try out. Walk up to someone you've never met before and say...

"Wow! You look great. I love your hair."

Note the response you get.

Then walk up to another person and say...

"You're an idiot!"

Then record your feedback.

If you habitually think great things of yourself, of others and the world around you, then you add to the greatness and nurture the world around. If you habitually complain, criticize and find the bad in others and in most things, then you are "rotting the rice."

More so, if you consciously speak certain words of hope, healing and victory to yourself, your children and family, you continuously release powers to heal and obtain victory in your life, children and family.

As a god of your own life, you can
create or recreate your life
experiences with your OWN words.

There's one more caution about words. When they are spoken, you can't withdraw the ones already spoken. Try as hard as you may to explain, the effects of the ones already spoken have been made.

In a Facebook post that has been shared over 650K times and gathered over 370 comments, Amy Beth Gardner of Cleveland, Tennessee, wrote about something special she did to prepare her oldest daughter for middle school. She asked daughter, Breonna, 11, to squeeze toothpaste onto a plate, then asked her to put the paste back into the tube. When her daughter protested, Gardner told her to remember the plate of toothpaste for the rest of her life. *"Just like this toothpaste, once the words leave your mouth, you can't take them back,"* she said.

Figure 2: Taken from Beth Gardener's FB page, to show what happens when words are spoken

Be conscious of what you speak to yourself,

children, and spouse. If you wish to achieve your all-time best health it begins by feeding your inner self positive thoughts of healing. Like *"I am strong; the joy of the Lord is my strength; I am growing stronger and stronger, I can do all things through Christ who strengthens me. I am unstoppable!"*

In this book, I'll walk you through confessions that bring healing. These words, spoken to yourself or to your loved ones everyday will bring great inner and outside healing. These words will empower you to walk in divine health.

Chapter 1: **Be Free From Guilt. Confessions of Forgiveness and Healing**

Kicker:

Inner guilt can be a great avenue for sickness and pains to thrive. Do not allow the enemy to fill your mind with guilt of sins you have committed in the past. Once we have confessed our sins, God forgives our sins and heals us.

Assurance:

"Bless the LORD, O my soul, and forget not all his benefits, who forgives all your iniquity, who heals all your diseases, who redeems your life from the pit, who crowns you with steadfast love and mercy

– Psalm   **103:2-4.**

Attitude:

Confess your sins to God, and then receive His forgiveness by believing He has forgiven you. God is not a task master who will keep holding onto your errors and mistakes. He forgives, heals and totally restores you.

Confessions:

1.

"The LORD God Almighty forgives my sins and heals my diseases. He redeems my soul from destruction and crowns me with love and mercy, in Jesus name.

2.

"I have inner peace and forgiveness from the LORD Jesus. My spirit, soul and body is strong, sound and lively.

3.

"There is therefore now no condemnation for me, because I am in Christ Jesus (Romans 8:1).

4.

"I have boldness to appear before God and receive salvation, healing, deliverance and restoration through the blood of Jesus Christ.

5.

"I am healed, hale and hearty; I am completely restored, sound, and strong, and blessed, in Jesus name.

Chapter 2: **Confessions of Healing From Offences of Men And Bitterness.**

Kicker:

We need to practice willful forgiveness of anyone we hold any offence against. When we forgive, we release those persons to God and release our healings and blessings.

Assurance:

"For if you forgive other people when they sin against you, your heavenly Father will also forgive you. - **Matthew 6:14 (NIV)**

"Bear with each other and forgive one another if any of you has a grievance against someone.

Forgive as the Lord forgave you.

- **Colossians** **3:13** **(NIV)**

Attitude:

Forgive because you love God, not because the persons involved have repented and apologized.

Confessions:

1.

"In the name of Jesus Christ, I exercise myself in forgiveness. I receive grace to walk in divine forgiveness. I forgive, not because I have been begged, but because I am a child of God.

2.

"Even as the LORD has forgiven me, I also forgive anyone who has offended me and release them to God, in Jesus name. (If possible, mention names).

3.

I receive freedom from any bitterness and hurt from offences of people. Whatever damage has been done to my health due to unforgiveness and bitterness, I receive total healing henceforth, in Jesus name.

4.

I hereby decree that I am healthy, sound and strong in spirit, soul and body.

5.

From today, I am abounding in love, grace and peace. I am rich in mercy, compassion and charity. I am healthy and prosperous, in Jesus name.

Chapter 3: **Confessions of Acceptance of God's Will.**

Kicker:

It is the will of God to heal you. That means that God wants you to be strong. He doesn't gain anything when you are in pains.

Assurance:

A man with leprosy came and knelt before him and said, "Lord, if you are willing, you can make me clean."

Jesus reached out his hand and touched the man. "I am willing," he said. "Be clean!" Immediately he was cleansed of his leprosy - **Matthew 8:2-3.**

Beloved, I pray that all may go well with you and that you may be in good health, as it goes well with your soul – **3** *John* **1:2**.

Attitude:

Accept that sickness and disease and pain are not the will of God for your life. If you have a child, do you enjoy seeing the child suffering? So much so, your heavenly Father does not enjoy your sickness. (Matthew 7:9-11).

Confessions:

1.

"Thank You LORD Jesus, for it is Your will for me to be healed. Healing is the children's bread. I am

Your Child, LORD Jesus. Therefore healing is my portion, in Jesus name.

2.

"My soul is renewed and prosperous from today. My body is renewed and prosperous. I have the life of God in me. I am walking in divine strength and health, in Jesus name.

3.

"Even though I am in human flesh, full of wrong thoughts and mistakes, I do not enjoy seeing my children suffer; how much more the Almighty God. I know that He is not happy with sickness and pains in my body. I therefore receive my healing

right now, in Jesus name.

4.

"I see the hand of Christ stretched towards me and bringing total cleansing and renewal to my body henceforth, In Jesus name.

5.

"God wills that I prosper and be in good health. I therefore reject any pain and sickness fighting the plan of God for my life today, in Jesus name.

Chapter 4: Confessions of Compassion of Christ Made Manifest for Your Healing and Health

Kicker:

God heals and restores our health because He is a merciful and compassionate Father. Here on Earth, Jesus healed the multitudes out of the abundance of His compassion. This compassion is still working today for our salvation, healing, deliverance and total   restoration.

Assurance:

When Jesus landed and saw a large crowd, he had compassion on them and ***healed their sick.*** *–* ***Matthew 14:14***

Jesus went throughout Galilee, teaching in their synagogues, preaching the gospel of the kingdom, and healing every disease and sickness among the people - **Matthew 4:23.**

And Jesus called His disciples to Him, and said, "I feel compassion for the people, because they have remained with Me now three days and have nothing to eat; and I do not want to send them away hungry, for they might faint on the way." – **Matthew**   **15:32**

Attitude:

Just like you are not happy when your children are unwell, so is our LORD and Savior, Jesus Christ, not happy when you are unwell and buffeted by the power of the devil. His compassion is available for your healing and complete restoration. He is the same yesterday, today and forever. _____

Confessions:

1. "Jesus is the same yesterday, today and forever. His love and compassion remains the same. His power and grace remains the same. If He had mercy and compassion for others in the Bible, He also has compassion for me and my family.

2. "This day, O LORD, I am a beneficiary of your compassion. Let Your healing power move in all parts of my body today, in Jesus name. I am healed and restored.

3. "The compassion of the LORD fails not;

therefore my health will not fail again, in Jesus name.

---

4. "What God does is permanent; my healing is permanent, in Jesus name.

---

5. "Thank You merciful and compassionate Father. Thank You God of love and peace. Henceforth, Your love and peace surrounds my life, day and night, in Jesus name.

Chapter 5: (The Power of the Communion) Confessions of Divine Life Through the Body and Blood of Jesus.

Kicker:

The Holy Communion is not just a church traditional practice. It is a spiritual symbol of connection with Christ. When we take the communion with understanding, we are connected to the life of God. Whatever cannot afflict the body of Jesus Christ cannot afflict you, the child of God.

Also, you can minister to yourself personally by taking the communion in spiritual reverence. It doesn't have to be taken only in church. You can administer it to yourself for healing ministration and   confession.

Assurance:

Then Jesus said unto them, ***Verily, verily, I say***

unto you, Except ye eat the flesh of the Son

of man, and drink his blood, ye have no life

in you.

Whoso eateth my flesh, and drinketh my

blood, hath eternal life; and I will raise him

up at the last day.

For my flesh is meat indeed, and my blood is

drink indeed.

He that eateth my flesh, and drinketh my

blood, dwelleth in me, and I in him.

As the living Father hath sent me, and I live

by the Father: so he that eateth me, even he shall live by me.

This is that bread which came down from heaven: not as your fathers did eat manna, and are dead: he that eateth of this bread shall live for ever.

- John 6:53-58

Attitude:

When we take the communion we spiritually consume the flesh and blood of Jesus. Every believer can believe God for his health and healing through the symbol of the communion. For your health and healing, you can take the communion on your own and speak God's Word over your health.

Confessions:

1.

"O LORD, by taking the communion I am joined to the Body and Blood of Jesus Christ. By the Body and blood of Jesus Christ I am connected to the life of Christ. Whatever cannot afflict Christ has no place in my system, in Jesus Name.

2.

" It is written in Ephesians 2:6 that I am raised up with Christ and seated with Him in the heavenly places, far above all principalities and powers, above sickness and diseases. In Jesus Name.

3.

"LORD Jesus, by eating your flesh and drinking Your Blood, I have eternal life working in me henceforth. (John 6:54). The life I live now is free from sorrows, sicknesses and diseases, in Jesus name.

4.

"From this day, the Blood of Jesus is speaking for me in the spirit. It is speaking my victory, health and complete restoration, in Jesus name (Hebrews 12:24).

5.

"LORD, thank You for the life that I now live. I am a winner. I am an overcomer. My life is free from sin, sickness and sorrow. I overcome by the Blood of Jesus and by the word of my declaration and testimony, in Jesus name (Revelation 12:11).

Chapter 6: **Confessions Of Healing Through The Passion of Christ.**

Kicker:

The death of Christ on the cross was not only for our salvation. It was also for our healing, deliverance and total restoration. This means that the price for your health has been paid years ago by Jesus. There is no reason why you should be sick anymore. The sickness in your body is a stranger without any right to stay there. You must reject it and mean it.

Assurance:

Isaiah 53:4-5 - *Surely our griefs He Himself bore, and our sorrows He carried; Yet we ourselves* *esteemed Him stricken, Smitten of God, and afflicted.*

But He was pierced through for our transgressions, He was crushed for our iniquities; the chastening for our well-being fell upon Him, and by His scourging we are healed. -

I Peter 2:24 - *Who his own self bare our sins in his own body on the tree, that we, being dead to sins, should live unto righteousness: by whose stripes ye were healed.*

Romans 4:25- *He was delivered over to death for our trespasses and was raised to life for our justification.*

Attitude:

There is no reason for you to be sick. You can place a demand on God about your health because Jesus carried your sickness on the cross. You can also command any sickness in your body to leave and it has no reason to stay, it must obey.

Confessions:

1.

"I believe in the death and resurrection of Jesus Christ. He was wounded for my sins and chastised for my sickness. Therefore, I decree that I am healed forever and ever, in Jesus name.

2.

"There is no debate about the death of Christ, so there is no debate about my healing and the complete restoration of my health, in Jesus name.

3.

"No sickness has a right over my body because I have been redeemed by the blood of Jesus. My body is now the temple of the Holy Spirit. And the light, which is the WORD of God and the Holy Spirit shines in my life, so I command every form of sickness and pain in my life to be destroyed right now, in Jesus name. **(John 1:5).**

4.

"Every seed of darkness in my life, I command you

to be destroyed by the fire of the Holy Spirit, in Jesus name.

5.

"I announce my healing and total restoration. I am healed and free from sickness and pain, in Jesus name.

Thank YOU Jesus.

Chapter 7: Confessing Your Authority Over The Devil, Sickness and Afflictions.

Kicker:

God has given you authority to command evil spirits and demons to flee. If you don't command them, they will continue to operate. But when you command them, they have no option than to obey.

It's time to stand in the authority that God has given to you and command whatever does not glorify God in your life and family to bow and leave.

Assurance:

Luke 10:17-19: *The seventy returned with joy, saying, "Lord, even the demons are subject to us in*

Your name. So He said to them, ***"I saw Satan fall like lightning from heaven. See, I have given you authority to tread on snakes and scorpions, and over all the power of the enemy. Nothing will harm you.***

James 4:7: *"Therefore submit to God. Resist the devil and he will flee from you."*

Mark 6: 7, 13- *"And He called the twelve to Him, and began to send them out two by two, and gave them power over unclean spirits ... and they cast out many demons, and anointed with oil many who were sick, and healed them."*

Isaiah 54:17:- "No weapon formed against you shall prosper, and every tongue which rises against you in judgment you shall condemn. This is the heritage of the servants of the Lord, and their righteousness is from me," says the Lord.

Joshua 1:5:- *"No man shall be able to stand before you all the days of your life; as I was with Moses, so I will be with you. I will not leave you nor forsake you. Be strong and of good courage ..."*

Matthew 16:19: *"I will give you the keys of the kingdom of heaven. Whatever you bind on the earth will be bound in heaven, and whatever you loose on earth will be loosed in   heaven."*

Attitude:

Bind the devil and command him to depart from your life and family and he will flee. Command every sickness in your life to leave and they will leave. You have the authority to do that.

In fact, if you don't do it, it will not be done because you are the principal prophet of your life. Don't wait for an external man of God. Arise and command yourself to be healed from today.

Confessions:

1.

"God has given me authority over the devil and his demons through my faith in Christ Jesus. I believe and confess that whatever I bind here on earth is bound in heaven and whatever I loose remains loosed. This is my heritage in Christ Jesus.

2.

"You devil causing pains and sickness in my body, I bind you right now and command you to get out and go into abyss, in Jesus name.

3.

"I cast out every evil spirit propagating sickness, pain and weakness in my body right now. I command you all to leave my body and go into the abyss in Jesus name.

4.

"I remind you evil spirits that my body is the temple of the Holy Spirit. It also written that in the name of Jesus Christ every knee must bow (Philippians 2:10). So you evil spirits, you have no

right over my body. I command you all to bow now, pack your loads and leave, in the mighty name of Jesus Christ.

5.

"I hereby decree a complete restoration of my health in hundred fold. I am healed of ----------------

----------------in Jesus name.

Chapter 8: Confessions to Enforce Your Spiritual Exemption from the Activities of Wickedness

Kicker:

Though we live in this world, we are not partakers of the darkness of this world. We have a covenant of exemption from the activities of wickedness. When others are saying "cast down," we shall be saying "lift up." When the land is being consumed by evil, we shall be spared.

Yes. We are spared from the terrors and afflictions that fly around. This is the promise of God.

Assurance:

Isaiah 60:2: *"For behold, darkness will cover the*

earth And deep darkness the peoples; But the LORD will rise upon you And His glory will appear upon you.

Colossians 1:13 - *For he has rescued us from the kingdom of darkness and transferred us into the Kingdom of his dear Son,*

Psalm 91:5-9 - *Thou shalt not be afraid for the terror by night; nor for the arrow that flieth by day; Nor for the pestilence that walketh in darkness; nor for the destruction that wasteth at noonday.*

A thousand shall fall at thy side, and ten thousand at thy right hand; but it shall not come nigh thee.

Only with thine eyes shalt thou behold and see the reward of the wicked. Because thou hast made the

LORD, which is my refuge, even the most High, thy habitation;

Genesis 7:23: *And every living substance was destroyed which was upon the face of the ground, both man, and cattle, and the creeping things, and the fowl of the heaven; and they were destroyed from the earth: and Noah only remained alive, and they that were with him in the ark.*

Ephesians 2:5-6: Even when we were dead in sins, hath quickened us together with Christ, (by grace ye are saved) And hath raised us up together, and made us sit together in heavenly places in Christ   Jesus:

Attitude:

Declare the Word of God over your life and family.

Though we are in this world, we are not of the afflictions of this world. This is the promise of God. Let it sink deep into you. Do not try to rationalize it.

Confessions:

1. *"I am seated together with Christ in the heavenly realms, far above principalities and powers, where I reign and rule as a king in this life. I live in dominion over sin, sickness and infirmities, and I've overcome the world, in Jesus name.*

---

2. *"By the Blood of Jesus Christ, I erect a hedge of protection over my life and family, in Jesus name.*

---

3. *"Every terror of the night, arrow of the day and*

disease that walketh in darkness, released against

my life, against my health and against my family, I

command you to perish by fire in Jesus name. _____

4. *"Because I am Christ, who is the ark of salvation*

and deliverance, I decree that I shall be saved and

spared from the activities of wickedness, in Jesus

name.

---

5. *"The glory of the LORD is risen upon me. The*

light of God is shining in my life, my health and my

finances. I shall grow from strength to strength,

from Glory to glory, in Jesus name.

Chapter 9: **Confessions for Total Restoration of Your Health.**

Kicker:

God knows that in the world we live, it's possible for you to suffer some loss. It could be in your health, memory, peace and finances. Whichever area it is, God promises you restoration.

Assurance:

Jeremiah 30:17 - *For I will restore health unto thee, and I will heal thee of thy wounds, saith the LORD; because they called thee an Outcast, [saying], This [is] Zion, whom no man seeketh after.*

Joel 2:25-26: *And I will restore to you the years that the locust hath eaten, the cankerworm, and the caterpiller, and the palmerworm, my great army which I sent among you.*

And ye shall eat in plenty, and be satisfied, and praise the name of the LORD your God, that hath dealt wondrously with you: and my people shall never be ashamed.

Isaiah 61:7 *- For your shame [ye shall have] double; and [for] confusion they shall rejoice in their portion: therefore in their land they shall possess the double: everlasting joy shall be unto them.*

Mark 11:24 *- Therefore I say unto you, what things soever ye desire, when ye pray, believe that ye receive [them], and ye shall have.*

Attitude:

Whatever the enemy has stolen from you in the past, in your health, in your memory, in your finances, shall be restored in Jesus name. Stand on God's word command complete restoration.

Confessions:

1.

"O LORD, I receive complete restoration of my health in Jesus name.

2.

"Whatever has been damaged in my life, LORD, let

Your Spirit work in my system right now and bring

a total repair and restoration, in Jesus name.

3.

"LORD, You said in your Word, that for my shame

you shall give me double. I therefore declare

double fold *restoration for my health this day, in*

Jesus name.

4.

"LORD, I decree that for all my wasted years, Your

power will work in me to cause immediate

restoration, in Jesus name.

5.

"Jehovah Elshadai, I believe that I am healed. I believed that I am restored. I believe that I have my breakthrough, in Jesus name.

Chapter 10: **Confessions and Prayers with the Oil of Healing.**

Kicker:

The anointing oil is a symbol of the Holy Spirit. When we minister to the sick with it, we can expect a manifestation of God's power for total healing.

Assurance:

Mark 6:13: *And they were casting out many demons and were anointing with oil many sick people and healing them*

James 5:14-15 - *Is any sick among you? Let him call for the elders of the church; and let them pray over him, __anointing him with oil__ in the name of* *the Lord: And the prayer of faith shall save the sick, and the Lord shall raise him up; and if he have committed sins, they shall be forgiven him.*

Mark 6:13: *And they were casting out many demons and were anointing with oil many sick people and healing them*

Isaiah 61:1: *The Spirit of the Lord GOD is upon me, Because the LORD has anointed me To bring good news to the afflicted; He has sent me to bind up the brokenhearted, To proclaim liberty to captives And freedom to prisoners;*

Matthew 6:17: *"But you, when you fast, anoint your head and wash your face*

Attitude:

The anointing breaks the yoke. Use the oil to minister healing to yourself and the same power that manifested through the disciples will be manifested through you.

Confessions:

1.

"Almighty father, as I anoint myself today, I command every yoke of darkness in my life to be destroyed in Jesus name.

2.

"I proclaim total liberty for myself and family this day. I command the power of God to move in my

body and enforce my freedom today and forever, in

Jesus name.

3.

"By this anointing, I announce that my healing is signed and sealed; my healing is verified and confirmed, in Jesus name.

4.

"I speak into the atmosphere right now; hear the Word of the LORD ye powers of the air, land and sea, whoever the Son sets free is free indeed. Jesus has set me free, so I am free indeed, in Jesus name.

5.

"God causes me to triumph in Christ and makes manifest His grace, knowledge and power through my life and family. In Christ I have the fullness of life. I have the fullness of victory. I have the fullness of health. I have the fullness of prosperity, In Jesus name. - **2 Corinthians 2:14**

Chapter 11: Banish Anxiety, Worry and Depression With These Confessions and Prayers and Release The Oil of Joy in Your Life.

Kicker:

The Bible says that only with joy can we draw from the well of salvation. So anything that fights joy and gladness in your heart is a sworn enemy of your destiny. Some of those things are worry, anxiety and depression. Today, you are going to release yourself from these enemies and enter into the rest that God has for you.

Assurance:

Psalm 45:7: *You have loved righteousness and hated wickedness; Therefore God, Your God, has* *anointed You With the oil of joy above Your fellows.*

Isaiah 12:3 - *With joy you will draw water from the wells of salvation.*

Psalms 16:9 - *Therefore my heart is glad, and my glory rejoiceth: my flesh also shall rest in hope.*

Proverbs 17:22 - *A merry heart doeth good [like] a medicine: but a broken spirit drieth the bones.*

Romans 15:13 - *Now the God of hope fill you with all joy and peace in believing, that ye may abound in hope, through the power of the Holy Ghost.*

Nehemiah 8: 10 - *..."Go and enjoy choice food and sweet drinks, and send some to those who have nothing prepared. This day is holy to our Lord. Do not grieve, for the joy of the LORD is your strength."*

Attitude:

Anoint yourself today and claim the joy of the LORD in your life. Banish the spirit of anxiety, worry and depression; and decree total restoration of whatever has been damaged in your life as a result of worry, anxiety and depression.

Confessions:

1.

"Father LORD, restore in me the joy of salvation, and fill me with the spirit of praise every day, in Jesus name.

2.

"*Let the JOY OF THE LORD start to overflow from the inside of me from now onwards, in Jesus name.*

3.

"*I command every spirit of anxiety, worry and depression in my life to bow, pack and leave this moment, in Jesus name.*

4.

"*O LORD my God, I receive the baptism of joy from heaven today, in Jesus name.*

5.

"*I anoint myself right now and decree that this is*

my oil of gladness. Let this oil of gladness heal and restore whatever anxiety, worry and depression have damaged in my life, in Jesus name.

THANK YOU LORD JESUS.

Other Books from The Same Author

1. Prayer Retreat: 21 Days Devotional With 500 Powerful Prayers & Declarations to Destroy Stubborn Demonic Problems, Dislodge Every Spiritual Wickedness Against Your Life and Release Your Detained Blessings

2. HEALING PRAYERS & CONFESSIONS: Powerful Daily Meditations, Prayers and Declarations for Total Healing and Divine Health.

3. 200 Violent Prayers for Deliverance, Healing and Financial Breakthrough.

4. Hearing God's Voice in Painful Moments: 21 Days Bible Meditations and Prayers to Bring Comfort, Strength and Healing When Grieving for the Loss of Someone You Love.

5 . Healing Prayers: 30 Powerful Prophetic Prayers that Brings Healing and Empower You to Walk in Divine Health.

6. Healing WORDS: 55 Powerful Daily Confessions & Declarations to Activate Your Healing & Walk in Divine Health: Strong Decrees That Invoke Healing for You & Your Loved Ones

7. Prayers That Break Curses and Spells and Release Favors and Breakthroughs.

8. 7 Days Fasting With 120 Powerful Night Prayers for Personal Deliverance and Breakthrough.

9. 100 Powerful Prayers for Your Teenagers: Powerful Promises and Prayers to Let God Take Control of Your Teenagers & Get Them to Experience Love & Fulfillment

10. How to Pray for Your Children Everyday: + 75 Powerful Prayers & Prophetic Declarations to Use and Pray for Your Children's Salvation, Future, Health, Education, Career, Relationship, Protection, etc

11. How to Pray for Your Family: + 70 Powerful Prayers and Prophetic Declarations for Your Family's Salvation, Healing,

Victory, Breakthrough & Total Restoration.

12. Daily Prayer Guide: A Practical Guide to Praying and Getting Results – Learn How to Develop a Powerful Personal Prayer Life

13. Make Him Respect You: 31 Relationship Advice for Women to Make their Men Respect Them.

14. How to Cast Out Demons from Your Home, Office and Property: 100 Powerful Prayers to Cleanse Your Home, Office, Land & Property from Demonic Attacks

15. Praying Through the Book of Psalms: Most Powerful Psalms and Powerful Prayers & Declarations for Every Situation: Birthday, Christmas, Business Ideas, Breakthrough, Deliverance, Healing, Comfort, Exams, Decision Making, Grief, and Many More.

16. STUDENTS' PRAYER BOOK: Powerful Motivation & Guide for Students & Anyone Preparing to Write Exams: Plus 10 Days of Powerful Prayers for Wisdom, Favor,

Protection & Success in Studies, Exams & Life.

17. How to Pray and Receive Financial Miracle: Powerful Prayers for Financial Miracles, Business and Career Breakthrough

18. Prayers to Destroy Witchcraft Attacks Against Your Life & Family and Release Your Blessings

19. Deliverance from Marine Spirits: Powerful Prayers to Overcome Marine Spirits – Spirit Husbands and Spirit Wives – Permanently

20. Deliverance From Python Spirit: Powerful Prayers to Defeat the Python Spirit – Spirit of Lies, Deceptions and Oppression.

Get In Touch With Us

Thank you for reading this book. I believe you have been blessed. Please consider giving this book a review on Amazon.

Here are other titles that will also bless your life:

www.amazon.com/author/danielokpara

I also invite you to checkout our website at www.BetterLifeWorld.org and consider joining our newsletter, which we send out once in a while with great tips, testimonies and revelations from God's Word for a victorious living.

Feel free to drop us your prayer request. We will join faith with you and God's power will be released in your life and the issue in question.

About The Author

Brother Daniel Okpara brings you the message of hope, healing, deliverance and total restoration. A humble minister and teacher of God's Word, businessman and lecturer, he is a strong believer that with God all things are possible.

Yes. The challenges of life are real, but with faith, you will surely win. Your health, relationship, and finances can be restored by God's grace and power, no matter how bad things are at the moment.

He is the international director of Better Life World Outreach Center, a non-denominational, evangelism ministry committed to:

- Taking the entire Gospel to the entire world, from village to village, town to town, city to city, state to state and nation to nation, in partnership with established churches.

- Training ministers, evangelists, and missionaries and providing them with tools, resources and impartation for the end-time assignment.

- Restoring the evangelism fire in the body of Christ through church workers' revivals and training.

- Producing evangelism materials and tools (films, tracts, books, devotionals) for rural, screen and world evangelism.

He is the host of Better Life Today, a Monthly non-denominational fellowship meeting that receives hundreds of people each month for spiritual fellowship, ministrations, prayers, business workshops, worship, healing, miracles and diverse encounters with God. He also co-hosts a popular radio and TV program, "Keys to a Better Life", aired on over

10 radio and TV stations across the country. Daniel Okpara holds a Master's Degree in Theology from Cornerstone Christian University. A strong believer in hard work, continuous learning and prosperity by value creation, he is also the founder of Integrity Assets Ltd, a real estate and IT consulting company that manages an eCommerce startup and consults for companies on Digital Marketing.

He has authored over 50 books and manuals on healing, prayer, Marriage and relationship, Investment, Doing business and Digital Marketing.

He is married to Prophetess Doris Okpara, his prayer warrior, best friend, ministry partner, and they are blessed with a boy and a girl, Isaac and Annabel.

NOTES

....

....

....

....

....

....

....

....

....

....

....

Made in United States
North Haven, CT
14 September 2023

41484115R00054